HOW TO WRITE A GREAT 'HOW-TO' BOOK

Become An Author Quickly and Easily!

BY: Lisa T. Douglas

Table of Contents

<u>Dedication:</u>

This book is dedicated to my loving husband and children, my true magnum opus.

Thank you!

I love writing, but you are the true fulfillment of my dreams. Without you, life would be unbearable.

I love you more than you could ever know.

Introduction

~ Anybody can write a book ~

~ Writing it well takes knowledge and dedication ~

If you have always wanted to write a book but didn't quite know how, this book is for you. You will learn to write and format your book like a pro. If you already enjoy writing but want to do it better, look no further.

Why a "How-To" book? I have four very good reasons:

- They are quick and easy to write
- They help others
- They allow your writing to be meaningful and successful
- They generate a quick stream of cash flow

Quick and Easy because you will be writing on a subject you know and are passionate about. This gives you a jump start to writing, requiring less research than if you undertook any other type of genre for the first time.

Helping others to learn is wonderful. Teaching what you know is the most caring form of sharing. Knowing that you are helping others will keep you dedicated to completing your book. Because you are giving a part of yourself, your writing will be *successful and meaningful* on a very personal level.

And who wouldn't enjoy *extra cash*? Our world has a thirst for knowledge. How-To books are flying off the shelves by the thousands and How-To eBooks are downloaded in hordes. Popular authors are earning substantial royalty checks and even authors new to the scene are enjoying a nice income boost. How much will your book generate? That is up to you and your readers. Find out today the tricks that can optimize your own income and overall success.

Imagine: Writing without frustration, ending writer's block and capturing a large audience...

Several popular authors who have mastered techniques I am sharing with you, have written their first drafts quickly and edited to completion with ease. You needn't spend hours sitting at your computer each day. If all you have is a few minutes after school, work, or soccer games, I will show you how to use those precious moments to your best advantage.

~ Even if you have never written a book before! ~

Writing need not be a big mystery and publishing a book isn't for the elite.

IN THIS BOOK YOU WILL DISCOVER:

How to write quickly and easily

How to create marvelous titles

How to quickly develop ideas into chapters

How to easily captivate readers and keep them engaged

How to edit like a pro

How to create a great book cover that sells

Are you ready to finally discover the secrets of writing a great 'How-To' Book or eBook?

The best is yet to come, so keep reading. Unlock your talent that propels you successfully into the world of authorship.

The sky is not the limit – the universe awaits.

Enjoy the journey. – Lisa T. Douglas

Chapter 1

Your Great Idea

"You have to write the book that wants to be written. And if the book will be too difficult for grown-ups, then you write it for children."
— Madeleine L'Engle

I am happy to begin this journey with you. I understand the wonder and excitement that awaits you. I recommend that you read this guide from beginning to end *before* you start writing, in order to see the big picture of creating your own book. Do wait to write, but never stop thinking about your book. Once you have finished reading this book, cover to cover, you will be burning to type. Let's not waste time; we'll jump right into brainstorming.

Your Topic

What is the best topic for you? Think of the many things you know how to do well and what type of audience this topic will attract. Discover what inspires you, something you would enjoy writing and your fans will have fun reading. This is the most crucial step in writing, because (let's face it) your final goal isn't to simply create a book, your goal is to write it well and *sell* it.

If you already have a great idea and just need the knowledge to produce it, congratulations! You have tackled the first big hurdle. If not, please read on.

Your great idea is out there – let's discover what it is:

- *Use your personal and professional experience as subject matter –*

You need not be an expert, but if you have enough know-how to instruct a beginner, then you have a fast track to success.

- ***Write on a topic you are passionate about*** *– Your passion will elevate your work from novice to genius and inspire others to become passionate as well.*

- ***Write about something appealing to readers*** *– A topic that attracts a wide range of readers is always optimum. Particularly for your first book, if possible, choose a neutral topic or something that doesn't provoke negative feelings or feedback. If you enjoy your topic, you will enjoy writing about it and readers will be more likely to purchase a book they can enjoy as well.*

- ***Is your idea new and exciting?*** *– Trends come and go quickly. If your idea has already flooded the literary market, heavy competition will surely stunt your success. Likewise if your idea is too out-of-date, sales will be sluggish. You can still write on such topics, as long as you are able create a fresh, modern and unique spin.*

- ***Consider the laws surrounding your topic*** *– If you are writing a How-To about political lobbying or building homes, realize that laws vary from state to state. Extra research may be needed or disclaimers added, urging your reader to know what laws or building codes may apply to them. It goes without saying, if you are encouraging your readers to engage in illegal acts, there could be moral and legal issues that arise for you and the reader. The best advice is to keep everything proper, uplifting and beneficial.*

Ask yourself:

- *What type of How-To eBook would interest my family and friends?*
- *What type of eBook do I wish had been written when I was first learning*

about...?

- *What is either a lost art or an up-and-coming trend?*

Perhaps you have several ideas that you think would make a great book but can't narrow those ideas down to one. Perhaps you are currently drawing a blank and have no ideas on what might be the perfect topic. The best trick I can give you here is to visualize who will be reading your book.

We often think we are writing for strangers, but who we are really writing for is people like us. No longer strangers, from this moment on, think of your reader as a dearly loved friend!

Know Your Audience

Understanding your audience will save you time and energy during your writing and editing sessions. Try to focus on what really matters – *them.*

Here are some helpful considerations:

- *The age of your reader – Different age groups have different interests, skill levels and limitations. Some material may not be suitable for younger audiences, such as projects requiring power tools or hazardous chemicals.*

- *Consider the location of your reader – This could impact how wide your readership will be. If you are writing a book that requires a specific location, such as hiking Oregon's beautiful Mount Hood or fishing near the mouth of the Steinhatchee River on the Gulf of Mexico, you may have a limited audience. Geography also matters when it comes to food, culture, weather and more. Every region in the country is tremendously different from any other on most of these points. You can be somewhat successful by writing a local guide, but reaching a larger audience will certainly yield greater returns.*

- ***Put yourself in your reader's shoes*** *– Try to imagine your reader and determine if your material is important to them. Why should they take the time to read your book? Will it benefit them and those they love?*

Tip: Try to put a face to your reader. Imagine pleasing them throughout your entire writing journey. Write as if their success depends solely on you!

Chapter 2

Streamline Your Outline

"A goal without a plan is just a wish." Antoine de Saint-Exupéry

The writing process begins with a jumble of ideas, all somehow related but not necessarily making complete sense at first glance. The simplest way for me to organize my thoughts is by outlining them, systematically ordering them in a natural flow.

I love an outline because it helps me include everything I wish and helps me easily see the things that don't really fit my goal. If I plan it like my GPS plans my trip to a new friend's house, I can arrive to my destination quickly and efficiently without having to go back and figure out where I went wrong.

I didn't always outline, instead I created the messiest first drafts imaginable. I thought outlining was a waste of time. I usually knew a portion of what I wanted to say and I intended to fill in the rest with my overflowing imagination – typing by the seat of my pants. Once my first drafts were finished I needed a clean-up crew rather than a polishing cloth. Being a 'pantser' created more frustration, writer's block and editing nightmares than I care to admit. I finally realized (and believed) that I didn't need to write this way, that there were methods that made writing easier and editing simple and it was time that I used them to my advantage.

Now my writing sessions feel very productive and satisfying – a huge change from my early writing years! My outline ends writer's block because I know what is coming up next. Writing is much easier because I can smoothly transition into upcoming bullet points. Another added benefit, outlining helps me determine if my topic has enough information to fill a book. I needn't find myself six pages into my writing, only to realize I have nothing left to say.

Some writers argue that an outline stifles creativity but what really causes a slump in my creativity is when I have to constantly stop writing to ponder my next point and research it on the spot.

All masters, from painters to dancers, use some sort of structure to help imaginative thoughts flow. Writing is no different. Planning, even if limited, lays the foundation for creating an easy-to-follow, cohesive book.

Once you use an outline, you will probably come to love it, simply for how easy it makes the writing process. Give it a try. See if you aren't more productive and have better results with this one amazing trick.

Here is how to do it:

Outlining the Major Points

You are about to create the skeleton of your book. Pull out a piece of paper and jot down all the major points your How-To process must follow.

You are not writing your entire book at this point, just putting your chapters in order. Think of this step as a very general plan as to what must be included and what is not necessary. Here is the original outline of the major points I planned when writing this book. As you will see, this step is only for my main bullet points; adding more details will come later.

1. Introduction

2. Coming up with a great idea

3. Tips to commitment

4. Outlining the major points

5. Adding more details

6. Expanding the details into chapters

7. Refining and editing your first draft

8. Creating dynamic titles

9. Conclusion – fame and a latte

Since my book is a 'How-To' about writing, there are no supplies or formal equipment needed. Your outline may include a supply list, equipment list and you may wish to discuss these in detail. You may also want to include pictures or illustrations, and other information specific to your core idea. Jot down the fundamentals you feel are important. When you are finished, look it over. Rearrange as needed. Add or omit anything necessary or unnecessary. The more general you can keep it at this point, the better. If your idea is best done in a specific order, great! This will make your outline as easy as 1, 2, 3. Another trick, if your idea doesn't require steps to be completed in order, try listing your steps from most important to least, or vice versa. You decide the flow that will work best for your reader.

Trick: Search online for books similar to your topic and read the reviews left by readers. Find out what they liked and what was lacking to tailor your writing. Look over their table of contents so you do not create a repeat of information, but instead, offer a fresh perspective.

Adding More Detail

Once your major points are finalized, it is the time to expand on those ideas. This where I see if my points have enough weight to fill a chapter. I want my chapters to be approximately the same length, so I can control this during the detailing process. For example, one of my major points may require significant amounts of detail and explanation, causing my chapter to be more lengthy than the rest. For this, I may wish to break the information down into smaller pieces, creating two chapters instead of one. Also, if one of my major points is too short for an entire chapter but relates well to another major point, I usually work it into an appropriate chapter, just as I did with *Outlining the Major Points* and *Adding More Detail*. Don't overthink this too much. Sometimes a chapter can run a tad long or a bit short, and that's fine. Again, you can decide which works best for you. Proper flow and content is more important than length.

I would like to note that while detailing, I realized that my final major point, *Fame and a Latte*, did not fit with my core goal. In this chapter I hoped to discuss giving back and helping others, something near and dear to my heart. While important, this message was off topic. Instead, as a better fit, I added information for publishing options.

Now, on to adding more details.

I'll show you my example once again. I took my major outline – the skeleton – and began adding some 'meat':

1. **Introduction**

   - *a. tell what my book is about*
   - *b. state how it will benefit the reader*

- *c. why I wrote the book*

2. Coming up with a great idea

- *a. write what you know – from work, from hobbies, from life*
- *b. who is your audience – age, demographics, skill level*
- *c. is your idea appropriate or trending – pick a topic that is marketable*

3. Tips to commitment

- *a. the will to do it – you are worth it, you can make it happen*
- *b. the dedication to stick with it – removing roadblocks*

4. Outlining the major points (now combined with adding more details)

- *a. why outlining matters – how it helps me*
- *b. creating a skeleton – general ideas, major points, list in order*
- *c. adjust when completed – add or subtract as needed*

Adding more details

- *a. example of my outline*
- *b. great time to do research on finer points as needed*

5. Expanding the details into chapters

- *a. write as if you are chatting with a friend*
- *b. make your writing personal to your reader*
- *c. add personality without diminishing the reader's interest*

6. Refining and editing your first draft

- *a. read your book aloud as you edit – engage both sight and sound*

- *b. correct spelling and grammatical error*
- *c. omit clichés, repeats and redundancies*
- *d. flow – use consistent voice and attitude throughout*
- *e. adding quotes or words of inspiration – adding pictures/illustrations*
- *f. hiring a professional editor*

7. **Creating dynamic titles**

- *a. hooking the reader – the importance of words*
- *b. catchy phrases that spark interest*
- *c. giving a promise and delivering*

8. **Writing your back cover blurbs** (added)

- *a. synopsis – an advertisement for your book*
- *b. about the author*

9. **Conclusion – fame and a latte** (deleted)

- *a. helping others now that you know the way – giving back*
- *b. time to write again!*

Add as many details as you need; every writer is different. I personally don't get too zealous here, I like just enough information to stay on track.

Look your details over when you finish up and see if it all flows nicely. Are you are happy with the content?

Before you plunge into writing, now is the best time to do any research needed. Take your time here – the more informed you are, the better. Add details from your research to your outline. You could also research at the beginning of each chapter, as long as it is separate from your actual writing sessions. Why? Well, for one, hopefully your internet is turned of during writing. Also (very important) is the fact that writing and research are conducted from different sides of the brain. Writing is creative (right side) and research is analytical (left side). Switching back and forth from inspiration to investigation is difficult and can leave you feeling quite frustrated.

You may also notice inconsistencies within your manuscript. When I've researched while writing, my style changes. My 'voice' suddenly turns clinical, and I am typing statistics instead of chatting with you, my dear friend. Dry data is boring. If I research long before I write, I come to the keyboard with a fresh mind, able to deliver accurate information without sounding like a dusty encyclopedia.

One last word about research – plagiarism. Never copy. Use your own words and tweak information so it is not a duplicate. You are a bright and talented writer, we want to hear from *you*!

Continue adding details to your outline until you feel you have a great writing plan. Don't scrimp here. If you need more details, add them! This is all for you and your success. You can add or delete details anytime – your outline is not set in stone.

Once you have completed your outline and the majority of your research, jump up and tell someone the exciting news. You now have the plan for your entire book, from beginning to end.

Time to sharpen your pencil and your wit – let the book writing begin!

Chapter 3

The Habit of Success

"The best kind of happiness is a habit you're passionate about."
— Shannon L. Alder

I desire to encourage your journey to authorship. All successful authors have one thing in common – they write! 'Not writing' is the only way you can fail on this project. To make your dream a reality requires your participation. The most important habits you can employ are **commitment** and **dedication.** Your dream *is* possible and you deserve to live it.

- **Commitment** – *The will to do what you have set out to do.*
- **Dedication** – *The will to continue doing it.*
- **Habit** – *The repetition of the two.*

Commitment

Make this promise to yourself, *"I am worth the work it will take to become a published author."* Say it out loud, stand in front of your bathroom mirror and look yourself in the eye when saying this. Repeat it everyday if need be. How long you write matters less than the fact that you actually take the time to write, each and every day. Every word is a step towards completion and success. Of course, the more time you dedicate towards writing, the sooner that success will be realized.

Dedication

We all get discouraged, but lack of motivation will doom any goal. You know this is true. Think about the last time you wanted to lose weight, start an exercise regimen, eat better, stop smoking or stop any bad habit and begin a good one. It can be really tough, especially when going it alone.

There is power and encouragement in numbers. Find somebody you can call and talk to when you get down and out. Enlist the aid of a cheerleader, perhaps a fellow writer. Promise to text him or her each day when you have finished your writing session. Accountability is a fabulous motivator.

Our greatest enemy here is usually ourselves. We make excuses and needlessly fill our calendars. We reason away the need to write today or decide that our extra long session yesterday covers today as well. Lies – *don't believe them!* The only person you are cheating is yourself. Be your own motivator and reward yourself with praise and possibly a nibble of fine dark chocolate every time you push forward. Every five minutes, commit to another five minutes, until your writing session time is fulfilled.

Great tips to stay on track during your writing sessions:

- ***Turn off your phone*** – *The temptation is great, so turn it off or silence it and put it in another room.*

- ***Turn off your internet*** – *Stay off Facebook, email, Pinterest and Twitter. Close all computer games (yes, even Bejeweled!). Remember your goal – to write on, right now!*

- ***Set a timer*** – *Writing under pressure can be very motivating and ends the need to watch the clock.*

- ***Write away from home*** – *Treat this time as your 'job'. If 'going' to work is best for you, then by all means GO. It is your career and paycheck at stake. Being away can also help with the chore and food temptations that you may fight at home. When out in a public space, ward off interruptions by wearing headphones and keeping your eyes* *on your own computer screen.*

- ***Guard your sightline*** – *Find a spot with minimal distractions and interruptions. If coffee shops cause you to people watch, write in a closet or room with no window. If you enjoy writing outside, turn your back to those sweeping mountain views or the busy bird feeder that fascinates you. I have found a fantastic hideaway in my dark garage, writing away in the comfort of my Ford Excursion. Rarely do the kids think of finding me there! One note, if you plan to write in your garage, crack a window in your car on stifling hot days and bundle up with blankets on chilly winter days. Keep the engine off – asphyxiation does not a successful writer make!*

- ***Take care of needs before sitting down*** – *Attend to drinks, restroom, pets, food, exercise, chores, etc. BEFORE your scheduled writing time.*

- ***Don't let your mind wander*** – *Even if you have writer's block, do not start thinking of what you'll eat for dinner or what you are wearing to next week's party. Write something – anything, even if it seems rotten, even if you feel stuck – fake it now, make it great later.*

- ***Intend imperfection*** – *Perfectionism will paralyze you, it will degrade your ability to produce. It will ultimately defeat you with the idea that you are never going to be good enough which means that your book will never be good enough. Those are lies. Editing will eliminate blatant mistakes. Remember that editing will come **after** your first draft is complete so resist the urge to go back and read and edit until then.*

- ***Use dictation software*** – *If you hate typing, hopefully you enjoy talking. Get dictation software that writes for you, or get a tape recorder. You can pay a friend or writing service to type it all up for you later. You can still be an author even if you haven't mastered the keyboard.*

- ***End fidgeting*** – *I admit, I can't sit still for long. I have to stretch during a long movie and sometimes pace when thinking. If this sounds like you, try writing at a tall counter where you can stand up rather than sitting at a desk. Take a few minutes to exercise just prior to your writing sessions – take a walk (gulp in that fresh air!), perform jumping jacks or run on the treadmill. Do anything that gets your blood flowing and releases pent up energy.*

- ***Pretend your chair is made of Velcro*** – *For those who enjoy sitting while typing, do not get up for any reason. Your body must learn to comply to your writing time. You are stuck to your seat, period.*

- ***Walk away*** – *Probably the best tip I have for fanning the writing flame is to walk away from your project at the end of your writing session. That unfinished sentence or paragraph will leave you enthusiastic about writing the next day. Tear yourself away but never stop thinking!*

Great tips to stay committed even when you are not writing:

- ***Think about your book*** – *Even when writing is not possible, consider your next words and how to say them well. This will help make your next writing session be more productive.*

- ***Read a book similar to the one you are writing*** – *My favorite mode of inspiration is reading. I love to read anything and everything and I do it daily, especially just prior to writing. Sometimes I opt for a book on a similar topic to the one I am writing, but not always. This habit familiarizes me with good format and inspiring writing styles. If your brain ever goes numb from writer's block, read a book.*

Research during non-writing times – *You needn't be a know-it-all to write a* *great book; that's what research is for. You can have a passion for something you know little about and your 'yearn to learn' can help you create a phenomenal read. Take notes to be used during your writing sessions (remember, your internet is turned off while you are creatively writing – so no research then!).*

Use these handy tips to write strong and finish quickly!

Chapter 4

Write Now!
A Fast and Easy First Draft

If my doctor told me I had only six minutes to live, I wouldn't brood. I'd type a little faster. ~Isaac Asimov

Writing. That one little word that both excites and scares every new author. Writing makes us vulnerable and complete all in one wonderfully frightening swoop. It grows us, makes us uncomfortable, interrupts life and defines us like nothing else can. Every time we place a word on that page, we share a little piece of our souls.

Beginning a new book is exhilarating. I like to start by giving my project a goal – a 'working title'. Not necessarily the title that will ultimately appear on the final draft, but the idea of what I want my book to be about. Here's my example from writing this book.

At the center top, using bold uppercase lettering, I labeled my manuscript in this manner:

HOW TO WRITE A GREAT HOW TO BOOK

Metaphorically, typing my titles this way truly inspires me.

- ***Bold*** *lettering implies the importance of this book to me. Without excuses, I will be bold when tackling this project. Nothing is going to stop me – not even me!*

- ***Centering*** *my title signifies my intention to remain focused until the book is complete. Also, to remain true to my topic, avoiding impulses* *to jabber about things that have little or nothing to do with my subject. The more focused I am, the better my first draft will be.*

You may have specific ideas to help blossom your own inspiration. Use them all. You are in the process of making your dreams come true.

Writing your book, from this point on, should be fun and easy. You may run into some trouble areas, but remember, you've got a good plan to follow and you *will* be successful.

You've already completed the hard part, dissecting and detailing your subject with your outline. All that remains is to expand upon those established bullet points.

Here are some great tips many experts use at this stage:

- *Write as if you are chatting with a friend* – *Relax and enjoy your writing. Allow your ideas and steps to flow like conversation.*

- *Make your writing personal to your reader* – *Pretend you are writing for only one reader. Use terms such as 'you' instead of 'you guys' or 'we' or 'us'. Most people read alone and really want to feel like your book relates to them as an individual. Give this person a name if you wish, put a picture near your computer. Type like you are writing just for her or him.*

- *Add personality without diminishing the reader's interest* – *Use encouraging text that draws your reader in, but doesn't add information unrelated to your subject. Too many metaphors, jokes or silly stories will bore or frustrate most readers. Readers **do** enjoy learning about your own personal experiences on your topic, and even the mistakes you've made along the way. Adding how you resolved issues is beneficial and tremendously interesting.*

- *Resist the urge to edit until your entire first draft is complete* – *I* *mentioned this briefly earlier but I know how difficult 'not editing' can be. It is a fatal flaw that you **must** overcome if you ever want to finish your book. It is okay to correct a word or two, but the goal of your first draft is not perfection. In fact, Ernest Hemingway eloquently acknowledged the that everyone's first draft is terrible (paraphrased). Like research, editing also engages the analytical (left) side of your brain, which means the creative (right) side is immediately turned off. If you constantly edit, you will produce little. After weeks or months of rereading and retyping, you will most likely end up with only one over-edited chapter, that you are still unhappy with. Perfection is subjective, likely to change with your hormone levels and moon cycles. What seems perfect on an 'up day' may seem fake and empty on a 'down day.' Believe me, writing for perfection is tedious and boring! Many manuscripts and screenplays are rejected for this very reason. While the story idea may be amazing, the spelling, grammar and formatting flawless, your book may be rejected because the over processed text put the agent or editor to sleep by page two. Sadly, this work, that will likely end up in the editor's trashcan, used up a good chunk out of your life and the original draft was probably much more interesting than the final product. Editing is a necessary step, but not at this stage. Trust me – just write, baby, write!*

Here is an easy way to complete your first draft:

- *On your computer document, type your outline. Place it directly under your BOLD working title. Take the first key idea and label it 'Chapter 1'. Expand on your major point using all of those great details you've thought of and continue until your first chapter 'feels' complete. This will not be your final writing, but don't stop to edit it yet. It is good enough for now. Once finished, move on to your next chapter.*

- *Continue this process, item by item, chapter by chapter until your entire first draft is complete.*

- *Stay in your chair and write every day until your writing session is over – your messy closet and errand running can wait!*

Once your first draft is finished, celebrate. Tell your friends and family. Pat yourself on the back for completing this major hurdle.

Chapter 5

Editing For Publication

I'm not a very good writer, but I'm an excellent rewriter. ~James Michener

Proofread carefully to see if you any words out. ~Author Unknown

Now is the part you've been itching to get at – correcting mistakes. This vital process will make your manuscript the best that it can be. You may need to repeat these steps several times until you are completely satisfied with the finished product.

Here is what I recommend:

- *Save your draft to a thumb drive, disc or back-up drive. Back up after each edit session. Learn from my own tragic experience. I lost a completed 80,000 word, half-edited novel draft when my hard drive was invaded by a nasty virus. My files were wiped clean and the hard drive was a zombie – seemingly alive, but no brain function. Yes I had anti-virus software and I tried to retrieve my work, but to no avail. I know I should have backed it up but, ugh...yes, I am still bitter...*

- *Read out loud when editing. Your ears are a fantastic tool! What you see and what you hear can sometimes be very different. As you listen to your text, you will realize instantly if a sentence works or needs revision.*

- *Remove any overused phrases such as clichés, metaphors, repetitions and redundancies.*

- *Make your sentences tight without removing personality. Reword to omit unnecessary words, but find the fine balance between robotic and rambling. If you can say that ten word sentence by using five creative words, without losing the meaning, do it! Your professional presentation will be more enjoyable to your reader.*

- *Grab a thesaurus. Replace ordinary words with charming, illustrious words. Resist throwing in those nine-syllable tongue twisters that force readers to run for the dictionary. You do not want them putting your book down – keep them engaged.*

- *Correct all spelling, punctuation, and grammar errors.*

- *Remove or replace all potentially offensive language or statements.*

- *Make sure your format is consistent throughout the book. If you underlined the heading of chapter one, underline the heading all chapters. I italicized bullet points, and made sure I kept this format style throughout. Formatting, in general, is a personal preference. If you decide to publish conventionally, your editor may have you tweak your work to their standards, but for now, do what works best for your book. Changes can be made later, after you sign that publishing contract.*

- *Make sure your 'voice' sounds the same from beginning to end, that you have used consistent enthusiasm, attitude and style throughout the book.*

- *Adding quotes, words of inspiration, and pictures or illustrations can add interest or humor for your reader. For quotes, always include the author's name. Pictures and illustrations can enhance or ruin your book. Research this topic thoroughly or hire a professional to ensure you get it right. It will be time or money well spent.*

Once you are thrilled with your edited manuscript, do one final check and use spell check. Print it off, double-spaced (to note any changes) and read through it one last time. I am always amazed how many mistakes I find on the printed page versus the computer screen I've stared at for days. Take your printed edited copy back to your computer to update and save changes.

Your next step is to have others read it. I print off double-spaced copies and ask my personal editors to use a red pen (or a black pen in conjunction with a highlighter) for notes. This way I can easily see their comments and changes.

Beg these trusted souls to be honest with your work and then show appreciation for all the good and negative comments they make. Find people who might challenge your wording – like a teacher, English geek or grammar Nazi. Stop avoiding (for now) that Facebook friend who spots every typing mistake – choose them!

Finally, decide if you wish to pay a professional editor. If so, use someone who comes recommended as all editors are not created equal. Again, this can be money well spent, especially if you've only gotten glowing reactions from friends who are too kind to offer negative feedback.

This part may take longer than you like, but stick with it. You will be glad you did. When you are pleased with your work, don't upload it to Amazon or send off that query letter just yet. There is one final step to success and it's all about fishing!

Chapter 6

Hooks – Creating Dynamic Titles

The difference between the almost right word and the right word is really a large matter — it's the difference between the lightning bug and the lightning. – Mark Twain

Hooks, lines and lures are not only essential in fishing, but also in writing and marketing in general. In your How-To book, you need to include *hooks* in vital areas, using effectively placed *lines* to *lure* your reader in. The main hooks we will focus on for now are the titles for your book and chapters.

The next time you are at the grocery store, take time to look at magazine covers. Those outlandish one-liners ("Queen Evicted From Buckingham Palace!") are all 'hooks' and while we usually roll our eyes, we secretly long to pick up that tabloid and read that highly entertaining and exaggerated article inside. We know it's mostly bunk, but we're *hooked*!

Your hooks will hopefully be just as intriguing, yet a bit different. Because your first concern is for the reader and being a credible, accurate author, we'll pass on the temptation to be outlandish. Let's look at creating legitimate, effective hooks.

There is a slight difference between book titles and chapter titles so I'll break these down separately.

Creating Tantalizing Book Titles

Your book title is intended to announce the goal of your book. My title, "How To Write a Great 'How-To' Book – Become an Author Quickly and Easily" isn't about fluff or fancy wordage. Simple words, if chosen well, can be extremely impactful. Why did I choose this title?

- *It fills an empty void – There are hundreds of writing books on the market today, and hundreds of 'How-To' books, but I could not find even one that instructed new writers how to write a 'How-To' book of their own. Finding a new niche gives any title a great hook.*
- **It's Catchy** *– The repetition is memorable and interesting.*
- *It's delivers a desirable promise – With busy schedules and demanding responsibilities, none of us have time for 'Drawn out and Difficult.' Give your readers something to hope for and make the process simple enough to achieve without losing too much sleep.*

NOTE: While I use the word 'promise' it is no guarantee. I can present you with knowledge, but you are the only one that can keep that promise to yourself to actually use it.. I can't monitor your time or habits, but I can encourage you. If you remember that the power of success is not found in any book – the power is within *you* – nothing can stop you!

Here are some expert tips for creating eye-grabbing book titles:

- *Make an exciting statement about your product – Like an advertising slogan with the 'product' being your idea, sum up the offering in a few clever words.*

- *Give honest hope – Using words such as, 'fast and easy,' 'in ten quick* steps,' or 'in 24 hours or less' promises accelerated results – something everyone desires. Don't say it if it isn't true, but if it is, boast about it on the front cover.

- **State it simply** – *Try to keep your title and subtitle short and to the point.*

- **Cute can be confusing** – *If you have an idea for a cute title that does not state your book's goal, use a subtitle that does. For instance, Anne Lamott's, "Bird by Bird," would probably be passed by if you were hoping for a book on writing. Her subtitle does the work here, "Some Instructions on Writing and Life." Without this vital quip, I may not have ever read her wonderfully popular and helpful book.*

- **Search titles online** – *Find inspiration by reading clever titles. Here are a few that I found: "How to Be a Pope: What to Do and Where to Go Once You're in the Vatican" by Piers Marchant, "Across Europe by Kangaroo" by Joseph R. Barry, and the ever intriguing, "Fancy Coffins to Make Yourself" by Dale Power.   Notice, only one of these instructional offerings has the words 'How To' in the title.*

- **Use unusual words or phrases** – *Pick up that thesaurus again and start having fun with the English language.   Ordinary words can get quite jazzed up with very little effort. Avoid using overused words such as 'Dark' and 'Destiny.'   Again, using clichés is far too predictable and boring, but a clever twist on those well-worn words will appeal more to readers. Any title that hints at being old or out of style could mean death to your book sales. If your subject is new and brilliant, your title should be too.*

- **Create a title that sparks curiosity** – *Add suspense, drama, or mystery to your title, forcing a potential reader to open your book just to see what might be inside. 'A Sure Way to Find Hidden Treasure,' 'Survive* *and Thrive During the Next Ice Age,' and 'The Secret You' all draw out curiosity.*

- **Use alliterations** – *Words that begin with the same letter can be memorable. Some examples are "Some Smug Slug" by Pamela Duncan Edwards, "Wemberly Worried" by Kevin Henkes, and "Alliteration Again and Again" by Larry J. Kricka.*

- **Avoid rhymes** – *While rhyming helps to make the words lyrical, the majority of rhyming book titles belong to the children's literature genre. Unless you are writing a How-To book specifically for kids, try not to sound like Dr. Seuss or Mother Goose. While I did find a few examples for adult rhyming titles, none inspired me to crack open the front cover.*

- **Use homophones** – *Words that sound the same but have different meanings can be attention getting. An example could be to substitute 'Super' with 'Souper' if creating a cooking How-To. This trick can apply to many subjects – use your imagination! I love the clever title, "Suture Self" by Mary Daheim.*

- **Say your title out loud** – *How does it sound? Is it easy to pronounce? Write it down. How does it look in print? How would it look in a browser search? True story – I was naming my online shop "Bim Bom" but, since that was taken, I added the word "Art" at the end. I liked this title so much I bought the web domain, "bimbomart.com." Did you read that as 'Bimbo Mart' like my daughter did? After the laughing subsided, I dumped the "Bim Bom" idea and instead opted for "Uptown Avenue" and "Uptown Vintage" for my shop names.*

- **Be original** – *Search online to see if your title is already out there. If so, change it up.*

Tip: Once you are satisfied with your book title, share it with family members and friends for valuable feedback. Other ears and eyes can sometimes catch things you've missed!

Creating Captivating Chapter Titles

Chapter titles vary from book titles in a few ways.

- *Book titles should plainly state the book's goal, but chapter titles should tease just a bit, invoking intrigue with just a hint of mystery.*

- *While rhyming book titles are out, rhyming is okay for chapter titles.*

Choose chapter titles carefully, they will become one for your best marking tools – your Table of Contents!

Here's what readers are looking for in chapter titles:

- *Will your book answer their questions?*

- *Will your book have new information or personal experiences not found elsewhere?*

- *Will your topic really interest them?*

- *Will your book be enjoyable to read?*

Here is how many experts handle chapter titles, addressing reader's questions, yet also piquing the reader's interest:

- ***Lure with cliff-hangers*** *– Think again of magazine headlines. If you* read *'Immediately Change Your Life by Updating Your Appearance,'* you might feel it is something you already know enough about. But if you read, *'A New You by Saturday,'* you may wonder if there is a new product offering quick results. If you take the time to turn to that article or chapter, you are usually invested enough to read the first couple of lines. Hopefully you will find new and fresh information that keeps you reading.

- ***Tease*** – *Give a hint, not a synopsis. Most readers love a good scoop. 'Shocked in Vegas,' 'Finally Found,' or 'Crazy But True' are all tempting titles worth further investigation.*

- ***Use the ideas outlined in my 'Creating Tantalizing Book Titles' section*** – *Many of the ideas offered for creating your book title could apply here. Just make sure you add a unique and honest twist.*

Tip: Once you have created your chapter titles, create your table of contents. I created mine by simply listing all those great chapter titles in the proper order. This is a list that sells my book many times over!

Chapter 7

Thinking Outside the Book

> *"No, even the best product ain't gonna sell itself."*
> — *Daniel Vlcek*

Your book may be finished but don't put your computer to sleep or your wit to rest. It is time to design the front cover and write the blurbs for the back of your book – important tools that sell your book. These are your full page advertisements, grabbing the reader's attention, explaining why they should care about your book and why you were the perfect person to write it.

The Front of Your Book

Your reader has a choice to make when they see your book on a store shelf – to pick it up or ignore it. This might seem obvious, but what are you going to do to entice them to grab it?

Let's not forget online sales – how will you make your book the one that buyers click on?

Your front cover is vital to every sale and must make a good first impression. Grab the attention of in-store and online shoppers with some great insider tricks.

Consider these tips:

- *Research other books on your subject, what covers have they chosen? Discover what you like and don't like about those other covers.*

- *Will your cover stand out impressively amongst the competition? For my cover, I wanted my title and chic typewriter image to stand out. The colors are monochromatic and soothing. It is inspiring and effective and stands out next to the many bright covers of other writing books. Loud and bold does not always equal attention-getting.*

- *Are your graphics bright, crisp and interesting?*

- *Does your cover relate to your subject matter? It should!*

- *Amazon displays on a white background. Will your colors pop, blend in or be washed out? Choose colors wisely. You may really like the color fuchsia, but that doesn't mean it is perfect for a book on Africa. Subtle colors can be eye grabbing, especially if they are trending, unusual or arranged in interesting designs.*

- *What is the mood of your book? Bright, light and uplifting subjects deserve a comparative cover. Likewise, serious and somber should be reflected in the cover. Think of the feeling one might get from your first page or first chapter. Close your eyes and imagine a scene or color that portrays that mood.*

- *Find websites that offer low cost book cover designs. Most are easy and fun to use.*

- *Hire a graphic design artist. Check references or ask friends for recommendations. Ask to see their portfolio. If their taste is too far from yours, make sure they are adaptable before hiring. Also, ask how busy they are, and if their schedule can show mercy to your deadline. An over-booked graphics artist equals a late cover and pensive author!*

- *Design your own cover using your own art or photographs.*

- *Get permission from parents before using a minor's photograph.*

- *Pay attention to copyrights! Seek proper permission before using any copyrighted material.*

- *Make sure your photographs are the correct file size, are bright and incorporate interesting images.*

- *Include the title, subtitle (if any) and who it is written by.*

The Back of the Book Synopsis

One of the best selling tools you have is found on your back cover in the form of your short, well-written synopsis.

A synopsis is a short overview of your book, generally stating major ideas without giving away the finer key details. Give your readers a brief sampling, not a long rendition. Your synopsis should be approximately 100 to 150 words.

Here are some expert tips:

- *Use strong, clear language.*

- *Mimic the style of a book that is similar to yours – one that might interest you. What format did they use and is it a good one to use on your own book back?*

- *Make every word count. Use tight wording, delivering impact in as few words as possible.*

- *Use bullets to highlight key features.*

- *Use words that evoke images or emotions such as "Icy Tomb," "Clinging to Life," etc. Get creative. Use that thesaurus until the pages are ragged.*

- *Ask provocative questions, "Can you hear the voice of God?," "Are you smarter than your dog?," etc. Use whatever fits nicely with your own book.*

- *Keep it short but powerful.*

- *Add some bold lettering, italics and underline for impact.*

- *Use multiple font styles, font sizes and font colors.*

- *Add honest, noteworthy book reviews and quotes praising your writing or insight.*

About the Author

The 'About the Author' is a short biography, typically around 50 words or less.

Here are some things you may wish to include:

- *A brief overview of who you are.*

- *A sentence about where you live and who you live with (Relationship status? Family members? Pets?) All of this is optional. You needn't share private information if you don't wish to.*

- *Note some of your other writings – books, articles, papers. If unpublished, share some insight of your overall writing expertise.*

- *A professional picture of yourself.*

- *Use specific, pleasant language that makes a quick, positive impression. Skip the exaggeration or endless bragging. No need to list your entire history of accomplishments. Perhaps adding a quick, short note about significant achievements, awards or community service will be plenty to satisfy your reader.*

How are you doing? Have you finished all the steps? Is this a book that you would enjoy reading? Yes? Then great job! You are amazing!

Conclusion

I hope you have found this book enjoyable and enriching. There are many options for publication, find the one that is best for you.

Avenues to explore are:

- ***Traditional Publishing*** – *Using agents and publishing houses. I recommend starting with a current year of 'The Writer's Market', which allows you find agents and publishers looking for a book like yours.*

- ***Online Options*** – *You can self-publish immediately. Amazon (for Kindle books) and CreateSpace (for paperback copies) have wonderful guides to upload and market your book. Typically when I self-publish, I upload to Amazon which then prompts me to upload to CreateSpace as well. Both will promote your published book free of charge.*

Once you decide how you wish to publish, there is a vast amount of advice and instruction available online. There are YouTube videos and online articles that can help you every step of the way. Do a Google search or purchase a book on the topic of publishing to discover what is best for you. The important thing is to *get published!* You wrote this book for somebody and *that somebody* deserves a chance to read it!

Thank you for reading. Thank you also in advance, for writing your own great book. I can't wait to read it!

"We do not have to become heroes overnight. Just a step at a time, meeting each thing that comes up... discovering we have the strength to stare it down." - Eleanor Roosevelt

www.ingramcontent.com/pod-product-compliance
Lightning Source LLC
Chambersburg PA
CBHW070349290526
45791CB00003B/1491